D1444538

# THE COLLEGE AUDITION

*A Guide for High School Students Pursuing a Degree in Theatre*

## TIM EVANICKI

*This book is dedicated to the hundreds of students with whom I have been fortunate enough to cross paths. You are the reason I wake up each morning and do what I do. I measure my success based on your success, and for that, I am eternally grateful.*

*-Tim*

*"The future belongs to young people with an education and the imagination to create."*

—President Barack Obama

# ABOUT THE AUTHOR

Tim Evanicki is a Juilliard-trained vocalist, vocal coach, master class clinician, speaker, and audition coach originally from New York, now residing in Orlando, FL. Since 2004, Mr. Evanicki has prepared his students for college auditions, and as of the publishing date of this book, he has had a 100% success rate for his students getting accepted to a Musical Theatre, Theatre, or Music program at some of the world's most prestigious performing arts colleges. For more information on Mr. Evanicki, please visit www.timevanicki.com or www.thecollegeaudition.com.

# CONTENTS

# PREFACE

So, you want a career onstage in Theatre?

Are you sure?

No, really… are you *absolutely* sure?

I'd like to share with you a Facebook post from a friend of mine, that I always delight in showing to my students:

> *"Today I started a new temp job where I transport urine samples across town by bike between a doctor's office and a testing facility. Also, I have a Tony Award."*

If you can wake up in the morning and picture yourself in any other career in your future, I have two words for you: "do that."

Life as a professional theatre performer is uncertain, at best. You will be constantly auditioning, reinventing yourself, searching for your next gig, your next paycheck, and your next job to tide you over between shows. You will live in a tiny apartment in Manhattan, which you will share with several other people. You will have to, at one point in your life, make the difficult decision of whether you should buy groceries or pay your electric bill.

However, if you're like I was in high school, you wake up in the morning, after dreaming all night about performing, turn on your best Broadway playlist, hop in the shower, head to school, where you look forward to your performing arts classes, and to the the final bell when you start your after-school rehearsals, dance classes, voice lessons, and performances!

If that second part sounds like you, and that first part didn't scare you, then you're making the right decision to pursue a career in Theatre! Yes, the road is long, and difficult. However, when you're standing on that stage and the lights come up, all of those sacrifices and struggles are worth it. And like I always say: "*Someone* has to star in the next big Broadway show — why can't that person be you?"

In the pages ahead, I will walk you through the steps necessary to prepare yourself to be a competitive candidate when it comes time to apply for your schools. Much the same as it will be when you're in the real world of Theatre, nothing about the process is guaranteed. If you follow the steps in this book, however, you will go into your senior year with the confidence that you've done everything you could to prepare yourself for the most exciting, stressful, rewarding, and challenging time of your life thus far: The College Audition.

# 1
# PUTTING YOUR PARENTS' MINDS AT EASE

It never fails. Every year when I begin preparing students for their college application process, the phone calls start coming in. Parents who are concerned or confused about the future security of their kids will start calling to ask if their little star is good enough to make it on Broadway, or if they should consider changing over to a degree in business.

My answer is always the same: "Who knows?"

No one can say with any certainty that you are going to make it big on Broadway. I don't believe that making it on Broadway is the only way to measure success in this field! Here's what I *can* say, which a great deal of certainty: **an undergraduate degree in Theatre or Musical Theatre is an incredibly invaluable thing!**

11

If you or your parents are worried about not being able to survive with a degree in Theatre, remember you are currently applying for an *undergraduate* degree. Theatre and Musical Theatre majors acquire skills that are sought-after in a great many fields of business including performance and presentation, leadership, strong written and verbal communication, project management, creative problem-solving, and the ability to work under great pressure.

When discussing the benefits of an undergraduate performing arts degree, Dr. Stacey Watt, Pediatric Anesthesiology Fellowship Program Director at the University at Buffalo, State University of New York, and Chief of Services, Department of Anesthesiology at John R. Oishei Children's Hospital had this to say:

*"Education is never wasted. This statement has proved true time and time again in medicine. Having a degree will serve you in many ways and is a solid foundation to build upon when pursuing a career. Some of the best physicians I have ever worked with earned their undergraduate degrees in fields not traditionally associated with the pursuit of a medical career.*

*Degrees in musical arts and theatre are great examples of non-medically focused degrees that can easily lead into a career in the medical field!*

*Having experience and skill in public speaking and being able to demonstrate empathy are extremely sought-after traits in medical school applicants."*

I see more and more companies looking for Theatre Majors to become corporate trainers, brand ambassadors, public relations representatives, and any other position that requires public speaking, or being the "face" of a company.

I offer these words from Kathryn Tricamo, Senior Program Specialist with Wyndham Vacation Ownership, when asked how a degree in Theatre has helped her in her chosen career path:

*"My primary responsibility is providing program education for our owners. From developing content to facilitating it in a variety of learning styles. My performing arts experience has been invaluable to me in this role. I present in-person seminars, host online webinars, and assist with creating video tutorials. My background allows me to adapt and relate to each different learner and audience I encounter. Engaging and entertaining builds that much needed trust in order for my learners to be receptive and open to the information I am providing to them. Whether I am on a stage in front of 100 members, or online and presenting to 200 from all over the country - tapping in to my theatrical experience is vital. Stage presence, confidence, expressive body language makes a huge difference when you are face to face with someone; and being able to effectively express myself through tone and inflection allows me to translate my messages virtually and still make an impact."*

Additionally, I ask you to consider all of the careers in the performing arts that aren't just performing on stage, and relying on auditioning to find your next pay check. After receiving their undergraduate degree in theatre or musical theatre, there are next-step graduate degree programs in Arts Administration, Music Therapy, Drama Therapy, Broadcast Journalism, Drama/Music Education, Entertainment Business Management, Costume Design, Lighting Design, Set Design, Producer, Arts Marketing/Sales/Advertising, and more!

Lastly, parents, you have already taken the right step. You have picked up this book and shown the initiative to put in the work required to make sure your son or daughter is well-equipped with the tools they need to get accepted into a competitive performing arts program.

Reading this book will give you a working knowledge of the steps and terminology involved in the complicated process of applying to a college performing arts program. I strongly encourage you find a college audition coach like myself. There are many across the country to choose from, and most are available for coachings via Skype or Facetime. You probably wouldn't think twice about paying for a tutor to help your child prepare for their exams. The college audition counts for as much as 85% of the admission departments decision. Doesn't it seem like an investment in preparing them for that experience would be a good idea?

Though a college audition coach certainly is not necessary for the process, having someone with the knowledge that has gone through the process time and again with their students, can save you valuable time and money. Other than college audition coaches and teacher who prepare their students year after year, most people only go through this process once, and don't have the benefit of taking a second pass at it after learning from their mistakes.

When selecting your college audition coach, be sure to check their track record and references. Find someone with a proven track record of getting students into the best colleges out there. Find someone who has working relationships with college admissions departments.

Please visit my website, www.thecollegeaudition.com, for more information on online and in-person coaching opportunities. I can help you find the right list of colleges for you, prepare you for the auditions by finding and coaching you on the materials you need to audition, and walk you through the steps you need to know right through to deciding which college to attend after you have received your acceptance letters.

Whether you want just a little help and guidance, or you want someone to hold your hand through every step, I can give you the tools you need through online videos, live webinars, masterclasses, and online and in-person coaching and lessons.

Now, together, let's take a deep breath… and step out on that stage!

# 2
# LAYING THE
# GROUNDWORK:
# Grades 9 and 10

It's probably around ninth grade that you will start to know for sure that Musical Theatre is going to be the path you take in your life. It's about this time that you should begin to seriously prepare yourself for this path. You're in high school now, and the decisions you make during these years will directly affect your ability to be a competitive candidate for Musical Theatre programs, when the time comes to audition.

Since the rebirth of movie musicals in the early 2000's, and television shows like "GLEE" and "Smash," as well as the new "a cappella" craze brought back by "Pitch Perfect," the number of applicants applying to Musical Theatre programs has grown exponentially. As the programs become more competitive, the amount of work candidates need to put in to prepare has also grown.

My least favorite thing to say to a student is "I told you so." Heed my advice now, and save yourself the stress as the clock ticks closer and closer to your auditions in your senior year.

Just recently I received a frantic text message from a student who was in Boston for his Boston Conservatory audition. It read:

*"I just got a text from my friend who had his BOCO audition today and he said there is an improvisational dance circle... WHAT DO I DO?"*

My first response was going to be:

*"Step One: find a time machine and go back to your freshman year when I told you that you should be taking dance class twice per week."*

Which brings me to my first piece of advice: **Get thee to a dance class!**

Time and again I've seen a student with incredible vocal and acting abilities get totally annihilated in the dance call. To reiterate my previous point, programs have become more competitive. Students need to be true triple-threats if they want to be considered for the top Musical Theatre programs. In fact, more and more colleges are requiring a dance prescreen video that you send in with your application that you must pass before they will even give you an in-person audition. (More on prescreens in Chapter 4)

When selecting your dance studio, make sure they offer strong ballet classes that fit your schedule. It is imperative that you take ballet – twice per week, if possible. Yes, boys, this means you too. Ballet is the core of all styles of dance, and the terms and skills learned in a ballet class are used in all styles of dance. By the time you reach your senior year of high school, you should be proficient in ballet, tap, and jazz. If the studio offers a Musical Theatre Dance class, take that too.

Next: **Voice Lessons.** They are expensive. They are necessary. They are a wise investment. The very first thing that colleges will be looking for in a Musical Theatre candidate is a strong, dynamic singing voice.

Take voice lessons at least once per week, and never miss a week! When selecting a voice teacher, it's ok to shop around. These days, most all voice teachers will have a comprehensive website that lists their credentials. Look for a teacher that not only has experience in the field, but has a proven success rate of getting their students into Musical Theatre programs.
Be sure the teacher specializes in the Broadway/Musical Theatre style, but has a strong background and foundation in legitimate, classical vocal technique. A music director with a degree in piano may be a great vocal coach when it comes to learning new music, but it takes a trained voice *teacher*, with a degree in voice to teach you appropriate, safe vocal technique.

I speak in greater detail about selecting the right voice teacher for you on my voice studio's blog www.thevocaltechnician.com.

Often overlooked, but just as important as voice and dance for Musical Theatre majors: **Acting Classes.** Studying with an acting teacher either in a private or group setting will definitely give you a leg-up on the competition. At the very least, a basic understanding of the core acting techniques is a must-have for any performer, and the sooner you start, the farther along you will be when it comes time to audition for schools.

I strongly suggest finding a teacher or studio that will teach one or more of the methods that are tried and true: Adler, Chekhov, Hagen, Meisner, Spolin, Stanislavsky, and Strasberg. Additionally, for Musical Theatre performers, it is important to have some straight plays and dramas on your resume, just as for actors, it is important for you to have a musical or two on your resume.

In your free time, read or attend live performances of as many plays and musicals as you can. Now is the time to start building your knowledge of the standard library of plays and musicals. This will only help you later on.

**Learn how to play piano** (or another instrument) and **read music**! I'm seeing more and more, especially with schools who offer a BM in Musical Theatre (more on degree programs in Chapter 3), a piano assessment, written music theory test, or vocal sight-reading assessment as part of the audition process. If your high school offers a Music Theory class, take it! Students who can read music have a leg up on the competition.

Now, I know I've laid out a list of necessary training and classes here that all add up to some very costly monthly bills for your family. With a little research and planning, we can keep those costs down. The first place I would look is at your high school itself.

Many high schools now offer piano/keyboard classes. Take band and/or chorus to learn how to read music and improve your sight reading skills. More and more high schools are now offering dance classes as a physical education option. High school theatre classes will work on acting skills. When planning your classes with your high school guidance counselor, be sure these classes are included, and that will cut down on your costs. Check and see if your county has a Performing Arts Magnet school, and look into attending. A magnet school will include all of these training opportunities.

The only piece of the training puzzle that you will probably not be able to find in your high school is private voice lessons. So, as your parents' heads are spinning from the dollar signs, remind them that investment in your training is an investment that will yield exponential results when it comes time to apply for schools.

According to my friend, esteemed voice teacher Kimberly Saunders Randall, "The pre-professional student with a dedicated work ethic and the talent/aptitudes to aspire to musical theatre careers, the financial investment in voice lessons has been repeatedly demonstrated to yield financial returns of up to ONE HUNDRED THIRTY TWO times the dollar-amount invested (many scholarships totaling $120,000 to $264,000 over a conservatory career), as well as admission, in these competitive times, to America's top conservatories."

Once the school year is over, you're going to want to begin using your summers more wisely once you're in high school. In the back of this book you will find a list of some of the most popular summer programs. It may benefit you to have a general idea of which programs you want to plan out for your three summers early in your ninth grade year.

This pre-planning will benefit you in more than one way. Some of the most popular programs fill up quickly, and applications can be due as early as December. If you know well in advance where you'd like to go, you can work on the application and video audition process to get those out of the way early. Also, these programs come at a premium price. Advanced planning will help budget throughout the year so you can save for these summers. Your choices will range from a single-week program for a few hundred dollars, to an eight-week program that can exceed $10,000.

While you may find a program that you love so much you want to return every year, I caution you to reconsider. Diversifying your training programs can only serve you, as you will work with as many different instructors, professionals, teaching styles, and theatres as possible.

When selecting your summer program, choose based on the instructors and clinicians you will be working with, over the destination. While you may love New York City, there may be a program outside of the city where you will have the opportunity to work with more qualified teachers. If you're beginning to seriously consider a college, check to see if they have a summer program where you might be able to work with the faculty, stay at the dorms, and get the real "feel" of the school. I strongly encourage a pre-college program during the summer of your junior year.

There are also several masterclasses and camps that take place during the school year on weekends and school breaks. For this, I highly recommend looking into the Broadway Artists Alliance (www.broadwayartistsalliance.com), and the National Young Arts Foundation (www.youngarts.org).

The Broadway Artists Alliance holds one-day masterclasses and multi-day workshops throughout the year in New York City. Single day programs with cast members of current Broadway shows and casting directors take place throughout the year, and multi-day "camps" happen in the summer and winter.

Young Arts is open to ages 15-18, who are in grades 10-12 as of December 1 of that year. As a Young Arts alumnus myself, I cannot recommend this program strongly enough. Each student selected to participate in this program will receive up to $10,000 in cash awards (scholarships), take master classes with accomplished artists, become eligible for nomination as a U.S. Presidential Scholar in the Arts, and you are provided with a lifetime of mentoring and professional support. The week-long program called "Young Arts Week," takes place in January in Miami, FL.

Lastly, **make your training a priority.** As a voice teacher, I can tell you the most frustrating thing is watching a student with incredible potential consistently canceling their voice lessons because of other (usually performance) obligations. Yes, it is important to be on stage and there are great benefits to doing shows in high school. But please remember: even though getting the lead in your high school production seems like the most important thing in the world right now, your training that will get you into the college of your dreams is more important.

# 3
# TIME TO GET TO WORK: GRADE 11

Congratulations! You're a Junior! Since you have heeded my advice from beginning in your freshman year, you are now at least on your third year of private voice lessons, you are a proficient dancer with a strong ballet foundation, you regularly read plays and work on monologues with your acting coach, and you can play piano and read music like a pro!

No?

Don't worry, there's still time. Getting a late start is no reason to panic. Your junior year is much of the same focusing on your training, with a few added tasks.

Before moving forward any further, we should talk about your social media and online presence for a moment. Social media has completely changed the culture in high schools in the United States by giving students a platform to communicate with each other in a public forum by sharing thoughts, opinions, and pictures of what you ate for breakfast last Thursday. Colleges know this. They WILL look for you on social media. Take some time right before you go into your junior year to clean up your social media. Make your profiles private. Make sure that anything that is visible to general public doesn't paint you as a partier, overly-opinionated, super-political, careless... you get the idea.

I would suggest changing your profile pictures to a current headshot. Cover photos and public photos should be of you performing or any other photos that cannot be perceived as controversial, illegal, or immoral. For instance, a perfectly harmless photo of you laughing with friends, holding red cups full of soda may seem innocent enough, but to a college admissions person, those red cups at a party might look like they have alcohol in them, especially if it looks like you're having a *really* good time.

Having a full year of being careful about what is out there on social media is a good way to make sure that there isn't anything you don't want colleges to see when it comes time to submit applications your senior year.

In addition to your social media presence, it's time to update your email address, if necessary. While you were probably very proud of your "harrypottersgirlfriend@aol.com" email address in middle school, it might be time to update to a more grown-up email address before we start contacting colleges.

Remember, your college audition begins at the first contact you make with the school. A professional appearance a demeanor goes a long way. Get yourself an email address that is formatted as "FirstNameLastName@domain.com," and be sure to use that email address at all times when communicating with colleges.

Now it's time to start thinking about and looking at colleges. The first thing you should do is make a list of what you're looking for in a college.

You may want to get a copy of my "College Audition Workbook," available for sale on my website. It will help you step by step though the process of college auditions, from selecting schools, to selecting repertoire, to choosing which college to attend after the acceptance letters have come out.

The first thing on your list should be which *type* of degree you are looking for. The three main types of degrees that are available to students studying Musical Theatre are a BA (Bachelor of Arts), a BFA (Bachelor of Fine Arts), and a BM (Bachelor of Music) degree.

The Bachelor of Arts (BA) degree is largely a liberal arts degree, with a focus on Theatre. A bulk of your classes will be in general education and liberal arts studies, with about 40% of your classes concentrating on your Musical Theatre classes. This degree is ideal for students who want to leave time in their class schedule for courses in subjects and topics outside of the world of Theatre.

The Bachelor of Fine Arts degree is a professional degree, where 80% of your classes will be Theatre-related with only 20% of your classes in liberal arts/general education studies. Students earning a BFA undergo a more rigorous training process than students on a BA track, and the end result is a more polished theatre professional with the goal of working in the field of performing arts. While this degree program may better prepare you for a life in theatre, your education will not be as well-rounded as a BA student.

A Bachelor of Music (BM or BMus.) degree in Musical Theatre is largely like a BFA degree, in that your liberal arts/general education courses are limited. The difference is a BM will focus more on the technical musician-side of Musical Theatre, focusing on voice lessons, music theory, piano technique, music history, and ear training. You will still have acting and dance classes, of course, but your liberal arts classes may be even *more* limited with a  BM as some of your liberal arts classes will be replaced by additional music classes. A BM is usually offered in a conservatory setting, or under the School of Music at a college or university.

Something else to keep in mind, while selecting your degree program. A BFA and a BM are considered terminal degrees, while a BA is not. This means that if you get a Bachelors of Fine Arts (BFA), you can usually only progress onward to a Masters of Fine Arts (MFA). In some rare cases, a Doctorate of Fine Arts (DFA) is now offered. The same goes with BM's only able to progress to MM's and DM's. Someone with a BFA, could not always go on to seek their Master of Science (MS) in another field.

There is one other degree that is worth mentioning, though it is not as widely offered as the others. A Bachelor of Science in Theatre is sometimes offered. The definition of this degree varies greatly between the institutions that offer it, so it is best to discuss the program directly with the school. In most cases, a BS in Theatre focuses more on the technical side of theatre, and a bulk of your credits are earned doing "hands-on" work inside the actual theatre, so it is considered "lab" hours, thereby making it a "science" degree.

There is one thing that all of these degrees have in common, according to every single friend and professional acquaintance I have asked who is in casting, producing, or directing shows: the type of degree you have doesn't matter at all.

My suggestion is always to look at the school's profiles online. Look at their faculty, look at their alumni, get a feel for their typical schedule, and choose program in which you think you will flourish most.

If you're a performer, the only thing that TRULY matters is what you show them in the audition room. So why worry about what which TYPE of degree you get? Well, this goes back to the very beginning of the book with "putting your parents' minds at ease."

The most flexible undergrad theatre degree is a BA. This is because a bulk of your classes are general education classes, so you can easily sail on to get your Master's in some other field. With a BFA or BM, you may be required to take several classes in math and sciences that you weren't required to take for your BFA/BM before you can begin work on your Master's. In some cases, you may even be required to get a SECOND bachelor's degree.

Is your head spinning yet?

Good. I'll continue.

The next thing you need to consider is whether or not you want a conservatory, or a more traditional "college experience." If sprawling campuses, Greek life, football games, and college clubs are important to you, then we need to be looking at a university program. If more intensive study, with longer days and less time to do outside activities is appealing to you, we'll be looking at conservatories. With a conservatory program, you'll only be looking at BFA's or BM's, and you will normally only take 1-2 classes per year that are not musical theatre classes.

Other important factors to consider is where you'd like to be geographically. Small town or big city? East Coast, West Coast, or somewhere in between? Is a senior showcase for agents important for you? (I say YES!) Only you will know what is important for you in a college, so it is important to make that list of what you want, then stick to it. Carnegie Mellon is a big name when it comes to Musical Theatre programs, but if that school doesn't check any of the boxes on your list of what you're looking for, then you probably won't enjoy your time there.

Recently, I had a student who had a very busy audition season, traveling to Unifieds in NYC, along with several on-campus auditions all across the Northeast and Midwest. When all was said and done, this student received acceptances from a few schools, then ultimately decided that she didn't want to be too far from home, so she decided to pick a school that was just one hour away. There is absolutely nothing wrong with wanting to stay in your home state when it comes to your college life, but a little more pre-planning and thought into exactly what she was looking for in a college, could have saved her family several thousand dollars on costly audition trips.

When making your list of schools, I have the strong opinion that you should not make costly "college visit trips" at this point. You will receive more rejections than acceptances, so odds are most of the schools you will be visiting won't even be an option for you. That sounds harsh, I know, but it's true.

Of course if you're already going to be in Berea, go ahead and schedule a tour of Baldwin Wallace. However, saving money isn't the only reason I caution against college visits early on. If you visit schools before you're accepted you may completely fall in love with a campus and "poison the well" for all other schools in your mind. I strongly urge you to wait until you receive acceptance offers from schools, the once you know what your options are, go ahead and visit each school. I know that goes against what your friends who aren't in the performing arts may do, but I would wager that your friends who aren't in the performing arts won't be applying for fifteen to twenty schools.

(Did he say TWENTY?)

Yes, maybe.

Now it's time to make your list. In the back of this book you will find a comprehensive list of all of the schools in the United States that offer a degree in theatre/musical theatre. They are broken down into three categories: Reach, Target, and Safety.

**Reach schools** are what most of you will call your "Dream" schools. These are what many consider to be the top programs in the country. They are the most selective, with thousands of applicants every year, and they may accept as few as eight freshman. I would break down that acceptance rate for you, but it would make you slam this book shut and throw it out the window. (Hint: it's well under ten percent.)

**Target schools** are schools that, while working with a college audition coach like myself, we take into consideration your type, talent, and school's acceptance rate, and we determine that you have a very good possibility of getting in.

**Safety schools** are schools that do not require an audition, but still have very good theatre programs. These schools you can sit down with your high school guidance counselor and determine which are right for you based on your test scores.

One more word on these categories before we get to the list-making.

This may be the most valuable piece of advice I give you, or anyone else during this process: *stay humble*. Through the entire process, allow those around you to remind you to stay humble. In fact, ASK those around you to remind you to stay humble.

Why?

Admission to the Reach schools, and in many cases to the Target schools, is a bit like winning the lottery. Yes, you can go through all the training and do all the right things along the way, but sadly, talent is not the only factor. Many times it comes down to type. Remember, these theatre programs need to be able to put on shows for the benefit of everyone in the program. They can't very well do that with a program filled with forty blonde sopranos.

You may have gotten all the leads in every show in your high school, and won every local (or even state) competition, but this is now competing on a national (in some cases international) level.

You are not the best. This may sound harsh, but keep in mind that NO ONE is "the best." "The best," doesn't exist. It's all about who fits in where. So where do you fit in? There's only one way to find out: Try!

A great way to meet with several of the performing arts colleges and speak to their representatives in one place is to attend college fairs.

The National Association for College Admission Counseling holds a specific performing and visual arts college fair that travels the country. This is hands-down the best college fair to attend, as there will be more performing arts schools in one place than any other fair, and the colleges will specifically send representatives from their theatre program to speak with you. At other fairs you may be meeting with general admissions counselors. For more info, check out www.nacacfairs.org.

Another great resource I have found for my students is **www.theatre-schools.com.** This site provides a searchable index for college theatre programs in the United States. You can search by major, degree program, geographic location, school ranking, and more.

One final word on making your college list. Ask for input from a reputable college audition coach. Perform a couple songs and monologues for them, and heed their advice when they suggest schools for you. It will save you a lot of time, headaches, and heartaches if you have some honest guidance as to where you will be a good fit.

## Choosing Your Material

Ok, moving on. It's the end of your junior year. You have your list of colleges. Now it's time to compile a list of the audition requirements and start searching for material.

When choosing any of your material, be it monologues or songs, you need to first think about your type. Know your type.

Be honest with yourself about your type. Ask coaches, casting directors, and workshop clinicians what they believe your type is, and trust them. Are you an ingénue? Leading lady/man? Character actor? Use your type to determine your materials, not just what you enjoy performing the most.

The wisest words I ever received in a marketing seminar were "the confused mind says 'no.'" If you sound like Cosette, but you look like Madame Thénardier, you're probably not going to get cast for either. Make it clear to the adjudicators that you know your type, and don't try to convince them otherwise. You want them, in your very few minutes in front of them, to be able to envision you playing several different roles. If they can't see any potential fit for you for a role, they won't see a fit for you in their program.

Most colleges will be asking for a contemporary monologue, and a classical. Unless otherwise specified, I would define "contemporary" as written AFTER 1900. Classical monologues usually come with more specifications from the school as far as what they are asking for. They may ask for something by Shakespeare specifically, or they may ask for something written in verse.

One word of caution when dealing with monologues, classic and contemporary: stay away from accents. If performing your classical piece, it may be appropriate for a smooth mid-Atlantic dialect (think news casters, and movies from the 1930's), but for the most part you want to show them who YOU are. A thick accent will muddy your audition and you won't walk out of the room having left an impression on them as to who YOU really are.

When choosing your songs, schools will generally ask for two contrasting songs, one of which was written before 1970 (in some cases 1965 or earlier). For your non-contemporary piece, I offer this advice up-front: don't wrack your brain too much on this one. The thing about music written in the past is that you're not going to find a piece that no one has done before, or that they haven't heard in the audition room. It's refreshing for them to hear the classics in this case. Stick to Rogers and Hammerstein, Lerner and Lowe, Bernstein, etc. It's important to find something that sits well in your voice, and shows not only range, but that you have control over your voice. Generally, the older pieces are the ones where you have more opportunity to show your technique.

As far as a contemporary piece, choose *carefully*. This is where you can have a little more fun and freedom picking your song, but make sure if it's not very well-known, it is easily sight-readable if you are auditioning in a location that uses a live accompanist. Check the school's requirements as to whether or not you need to bring sheet music, or a recorded accompaniment.

There are many great resources to finding the materials you need for your college auditions, but my first suggestion to everyone is *Performer Stuff* (www.performerstuff.com). This website is a great resource for searching for material that fits your type and the genre you need.

There is another fantastic book series that has just come out called "The Musical Theatre Codex," by Anita Anderson Endsley. The Musical Theatre Codex lists solos, duets, and ensemble pieces from 178 musical theatre scores dated 1925 to current Broadway productions. Songs have been assigned one of nine character types defined by The Musical Theatre Codex Theory of Theatrical Archetypes.

*Buy. This. Book.* There is a link to purchase it on my website on the store page.

Be sure to check each school's website for the time limitations for each piece, and strictly adhere to them. Some schools will ask for 16 bars, some will ask for 32 bars. Some will ask for 1-minute, some will ask for 2-minutes, some (rarely) will ask for full songs.

"But what if my song goes by really fast, and the number of measures they ask for is less than 30 seconds of singing?"

Good Question!

Use this as a general rule: "16 bars" equals 30 seconds, "32 bars" equals one minute. I have told my students to use this rule for fifteen years, and I used it for fifteen years before that. Never has there ever been any problem using this rule, from auditions for schools, to auditions for Broadway shows.

Be sure that your music is a very clear copy, with no smudges or blurs, and nothing cut off. Hint: if you reduce a standard music book size to 92%, it will fit on a piece of copy paper. Sheets should be in NON-GLARE sheet protectors, and put into a three-ring binder. Please do not use a binder more than 2 ½", as the ring gets to be too large to have the accompanist easily turn the pages.

Clearly mark the start and end of your music with a bracket, in thick, black ink. Write in any tempo markings at the beginning of your cut, that might not be there. Then got back through and using a highlighter, go over your markings you made in thick black ink, and also highlight any tempo changes, ritards, fermatas, and anything else you think might be missed by someone who is sight-reading a piece.

If there is no introduction to your cut, and you want a bell-tone instead, write "Bell-tone" and the letter of the note you want played as your bell-tone before you begin. (i.e. "Belltone B-flat."

You will also need to record your accompaniment tracks for each cut of your music. You may be recording 16-bar, 32-bar, 2-minute, and full song cuts for each piece, so before you start recording, please make sure you have your complete list.

Also note, that at least one college asks you to leave a CD of you singing your audition songs with the adjudicator before you leave your audition. Be sure you've done your research and you know exactly what you need to record.

Before you record your pieces, make sure you have found a professional accompanist, and most importantly, and *in-tune* piano. The good news is, recording these tracks shouldn't take long, so the expense of paying an accompanist will be minimal, and if your voice teacher plays piano well enough, then there may be no expense at all!

Don't spend money on a recording studio or equipment. Nowadays, every smart phone is capable of recording tracks that are a quality that good enough for this purpose. Also, you will most likely be playing these tracks from your phone at your audition, so recording them right on your phone makes things easier.

Make sure that while you are recording your tracks, there is very little ambient noise in the room. No horns honking outside, or dogs barking in the next room. This probably goes without saying, but you'd be surprised what I've heard in the past. Lastly, do not set your phone directly on the piano when you are recording. The vibrations will distort the sound of the recording. In fact, I suggest setting your phone on a flat surface on the other side of the room while you are recording.

Bring a portable speaker, preferably the one that you will be bringing to your auditions, and play the tracks back through that speaker to make sure they sound ok. Listening to them on your phone's speaker may not be a good representation.

Lastly, once the tracks are recorded on your phone, email them to yourself, and text them to whoever will be traveling with you to your auditions. This way if something happens to your phone, the tracks are saved in your email, and on the phones of the people who will be traveling to auditions with you.

## Headshots

The summer between your junior and senior year is the perfect time to update your headshots. These headshots should be a clear photo that above all else, should look like YOU. The photo should be a close-up of your head and shoulders only. Some headshot photographers will want to get a little more artistic and show you from your torso up. In my opinion, that is not right for this type of headshot.

Choose a headshot photographer that is very knowledgeable in actor headshots specifically, and not corporate headshots or portraits. A true headshot photographer will provide you with a CD or download of all of the shots taken that day and you will be able to choose which headshots you like best. I suggest choosing two shots. One more happy/smiley, and one with a more serious expression.

Keep your look clean, by not wearing much makeup (if any), and guys make sure that you are clean shaven or your facial hair is very well-groomed. Stick with solid-colored shirts that err on the side of conservative, and don't wear any jewelry that is distracting. Any post-production editing should only enhance the photo, and not cover-up or change too much. Again, the photo should look like you, and not an air-brushed china doll. One of the worst notes I've seen an adjudicator make (and I've made this note several times) is *"does not look like headshot."*

The headshot should be color, and be printed as a glossy 8"x10" print. Do not pay for expensive portrait printing. A simple google search for headshot printers should give you a list of several online (by mail) or local printers that will print 100 or more copies for you for a relatively low cost.

You may choose to print your headshot with a black or white frame around your photo, and your name should be printed clearly at the bottom. Be sure to pick a basic font for your name. Nothing with too flowery.

I have a collection of great headshots, done by my headshot photographer of choice, Michael Cairns (www.wetorangetudio.com), that I am happy to share with you, if you contact me through my website.

## College Resume

Your college resume should be a comprehensive overview of your accomplishments as a performer thus far. Nothing on your resume should be from before your freshman year of high school.

The top of your resume should have your name (large and bold), followed by your basic stats: height, hair color, eye color, singing voice type (if applying for Musical Theatre), as well as your email and cell phone contact information. Do NOT include your weight on your resume. A clear headshot should give them all the information they need about your body type. Putting a number to your weight on your resume can be misleading and they may remember you thinner or heavier than you actually are if you put your weight. Also, do not put your home address on your resume. Parents' names and contact information should also not be on your resume. You are eighteen now, and the school will contact you, not your parents.

Remember when I encouraged you to pick two different headshot looks? Whichever look is NOT the one you printed for your main headshot should go at the top of your resume, in a size no larger than 2" high.

The first section of your resume should be your stage credits, listed in three columns. The first column should be the title of the play or musical, the middle column should be the role you played, and the third column should be where the play was produced, or the name of the production company that produced the play, whichever is more recognizable. Your credits should not be listed chronologically like a business resume, rather they should be listed with the larger roles/leads at the top, down to ensemble roles at the bottom.

The second section should be your training. List your high school, summer programs, voice studio, acting studio, dance studio and any master classes you took. Be sure to list the teachers you study with. The entertainment world is smaller than you think, and any personal connections between the colleges and any teachers you have studied may help.

The last section, at the bottom of your resume should be a list of awards or honors that you have received in high school in the field of performing arts. List any adjudications, festival awards, scholarships, honors, etc. here.

Be sure to keep the entire resume no longer than one page. The page should measure 8"x10" and should be stapled or printed to the back of your 8"x10" headshot.

I'm including a sample of a good college resume. Obviously, the names are not real, and are somewhat comical, but you should be able to get the gist of what is needed.

# Abigail Auditioner

**Height: 5'6" | Eyes: Green | Hair: Red | Mezzo-Soprano**
abigail.auditioner@gmail.com | (555) 867-5309

Thumbnail of Second
Headshot Look

## Theatre

| | | |
|---|---|---|
| Oklahoma! | Ado Annie | Pearl Bailey High School |
| Jesus Christ Superstar | Narrator | Merman Summer Camp |
| Hello Dolly! | Dolly Levi | Pearl Bailey High School |
| South Pacific | Bloody Mary | Pearl Bailey High School |
| Shrek | Fiona | Carol Channing Theatre |
| Anything Goes | Hope Harcourt | Pearl Bailey High School |
| Les Miserables: School Edition | Featured Ensemble | Merman Summer Camp |
| You Can't Take it With You | Rheba | Pearl Bailey High School |
| Oliver! | Ensemble | Pearl Bailey High School |

## Training

| | | |
|---|---|---|
| Tim Evanicki | Voice Teacher | 2015 - Present |
| The Bob Fosse Studio | Ballet (Agnes DeMille) | 2015 - Present |
| | Tap (Savion Glover) | 2016 - Present |
| | Jazz (Susan Stroman) | 2015 - Present |
| Uta Hagen | Acting and Monologue Coach | 2015 - Present |
| Master Classes | Vocal Technique, Seth Rudetsky | 2014 |
| | Acting for Camera, Steven Spielberg | 2013 |

## Awards

Thespian Scholarship Recipient (2015), Drama Ovations Award (2016), Best Actor Applause Award (2017), U.S. Presidential Scholar in the Arts (2017)

43

## Plan Your Summer Wisely

As I have mentioned before, the summer of your Junior year is very important. When planning your summer before your senior year, aside from attending a pre-college summer program, I suggest students take one thing into consideration: their weaknesses.

Ask your teachers, coaches, and directors where they think you need the most improvement, and pick your summer training with those weaknesses in mind. If monologues are an area of weakness for you, I suggest attending a program with a strong acting component. Double-down on your dance and voice training over the summer and begin working on your audition materials for prescreens. Consider joining a gym, or attending a fitness boot camp to be sure you are in the best physical condition you can be for your body type.

As difficult as this might be to hear, this is not the summer to just audition for a show, or do a summer program that focuses solely on the production of a play or musical. Again, on-stage experience is important, but not as important as making sure you are properly trained and prepared for your upcoming audition season. These are the most important auditions you have done in your life thus far.

# 4
# SHOWTIME:
# YOUR SENIOR YEAR

*"It doesn't matter where you are in this journey of artistic development. What matters is that you share with us where you are in that journey and just be present and open to the experience of the audition. Just getting to the audition is an achievement unto itself."*
*-Chris Anderson, Director of Admission, NYU Tisch*

Before I go on with this chapter, I wanted to share with you that beautiful sentiment that Chris Anderson shared with a room full of auditionees and their parents at the NYU Tisch on-campus auditions in February 2018, that I was attending with one of my students. I feel that it is important to remember that colleges aren't looking for perfection. They are looking for potential.

You are about to embark on one of the most stressful and scary journeys of your life thus far. Just remember this: literally *everyone* is rooting for you! The college representatives behind the table *want* you to be the perfect candidate for their program. They *want* to find talented people for their program, and they *want* that person to be the next person that walks into the room: YOU!

## Acceptd

*Acceptd* (www.getacceptd.com) is a website that you will use and get to know very well throughout this process. You can sign up for an account whenever you'd like, but you will need to do it before you begin your applications. You may already have an account if you have previously applied to some of the larger summer programs.

Acceptd is used by most colleges, universities, and summer programs to accept digital auditions. You will use Acceptd to upload your prescreen auditions, and in many cases, to schedule your in-person audition times. Acceptd also can be used as a great search tool to find summer programs and college programs as you begin your search.

## College Confidential

College Confidential (www.collegeconfidential.com) is a forum website where students can log in with their username and password and discuss, in open forum different topics about the college application process in general, or discuss specific schools.

While this can be a great resource to find tips and information from students who have already gone through the process, or to share ideas and information that others have researched, I do offer some words of warning.

It is important that you verify any information you get from these open forums. "Tips" given by people who post in these forums are sometimes hearsay, and can sometime not be 100% true, or may steer you in a direction that may make the process of auditioning more difficult for you. Trust your teachers and coaches, and if you read something on the site, check with the school's website, or try to verify the information from another resource.

## Facebook Groups

The same goes for Facebook groups. These online groups can be a great place to chat with other students, meet some others that are going through the same process, and compare notes, but other students are not always the best place to get tips on auditioning. Remember, this is a competition, and at times it is best to keep your cards close to your chest.

## Prescreen Auditions

Because of the sheer number of applicants to their programs, many colleges and conservatories require a prescreen audition. A prescreen is a video audition you will submit to each school which will provide them with a sample of your talent. They will use this process to invite talent to audition in-person, or to weed out applicants that aren't right for their program.

Again, because of the volume of applicants, I've been noticing a shift in the deadlines for prescreen videos. Just a few years ago, I would still be filming my students' prescreen videos over their Thanksgiving break. Now I suggest students have their prescreens ready and filmed no later than early-September.

In most cases, the requirements for the prescreen audition videos will be the same as for in-person auditions, but you must read the requirements carefully to make sure. Select a well-lit room, in front of a non-distracting back drop (a blank wall is best).

I suggest following the same attire guidelines you will follow for your in-person auditions (more on that in the coming pages).

There is no point, in my opinion, to spend thousands on getting your prescreen videos professionally filmed. In fact, they shouldn't be over-produced. They should be simple, and as long as they can be clearly seen and heard, your talents should shine through. In fact, I've had students who have paid for a trip to NYC to have their prescreens professionally filmed in a studio, and students who have filmed them in their hours with an iPad, and both of those students got into the same schools.

That being said, if you don't have a good camera, basic video editing knowledge, and a good place to film, then paying someone a couple of hundred dollars to record your audition is a very wise investment. Each city will have many options to video record auditions.

I have a small video room set up in my studio in Florida. It is basic, but it's perfect for recording pre-screen auditions with a plain backdrop, a couple of lights, and a decent camera.

For a more in-depth video tutorial on pre-screen video auditions, please visit my website or follow us on YouTube.

## Types of In-Person Auditions

The first type of college audition that you will likely come across is what I call the Collective Audition. These auditions usually happen at statewide or national theatre festivals, where you will have one audition, usually 90-seconds long, where you will perform your audition in a theatre or ballroom in front of many college representatives at one time. Only in the rarest of occasions will you get a college acceptance from these auditions. Usually, the college will give a student a "callback," where they will speak to the student that they are interested in, and invite that to apply for their program. Sometimes they will offer you a voucher for an application fee waiver, or invite you directly to one of their on-campus or off-campus "official" auditions.

On-Campus Auditions take place at the college or university where you are applying. If you are attending one of these auditions, you can plan on spending 3-5 hours (sometimes more) there. At these auditions you will usually meet some, or all, of the faculty. They will often include an informational session for students, and a separate session for parents. Please do not believe the myth that you have a more of a leg-up on the competition if you audition on-campus.

Off-Campus Auditions are held in cities across the country by individual colleges. These will usually have the same process and schedule as on-campus auditions.

The National Unified Auditions take place in New York, Chicago, and Los Angeles during the end of January/beginning of February each year. At the Unified Auditions, several colleges and universities meet at one location to hold their auditions, though unlike Collective Auditions, you will be auditioning for them one-on-one in private studios or hotel ballrooms. These auditions are a great opportunity to audition for several schools in one trip, as there are over 40 colleges and universities that attend at one time. While not all are "official" National Unified schools, many colleges will also hold their auditions in the same building, or very close by during the same dates, or just a few days before or after. Auditions, dance calls, and callbacks happen all within the dates of the auditions in each city.

One unique feature of the Unified Auditions, is the opportunity for "walk-up" auditions. While it is imperative that you pre-schedule your auditions for the schools where you want to audition, you will have the ability in your free time at Unifieds to walk up and down the hallways and check in at each school's room to see if they are taking walk-in auditions. There are two important things to remember though:

1. The most popular schools with the biggest names, with almost NEVER take walk-ups at unified auditions.

2. Some of the schools will require an audition fee for walkups. This fee is usually between $25 and $75. Please have cash, checks, and a credit or debit card ready, as each school's payment options differ.

Though other college audition coaches have differing opinions, I believe firmly that you should be seen by as many colleges as possible at Unifieds. Fill your schedule with as many walk-ups as your time and stamina allows, around your pre-scheduled auditions. In many cases since I started coaching kids for college auditions since 2004, schools that were not on my students' original college lists became major contenders after they did a walk-up audition at Unifieds, and in some cases they chose to attend one of their walk-up schools. After meeting the faculty member at the auditions, or after the school showed serious interest in them, they began to look at some school options they didn't think of before.

I usually suggest you plan on attending two different cities for Unifieds. If you do this, you can usually get most, if not all of your college auditions checked off your list. Most of my students attend the NYC and Chicago auditions. Chicago is the largest Unifieds, and they take place in a large hotel, occupying most of their convention and meeting room space. Many, many schools and summer programs hold their auditions at one time in Chicago, and there is even a vendor area where you can meet representatives from schools and summer programs.

## Audition Attire

For both pre-screen and in-person auditions, I suggest the following guidelines when picking your audition attire. Though it is important that your personality and type are reflected in what you wear to your audition, it is important to follow these basic guidelines.

Keep your wardrobe consisting of solid colors, or at the very most a SIMPLE pattern. Stay away from black, white, or gray. I'm also going to add burgundy to this list. Why, you ask? For whatever reason it always seems like more than half of the students auditioning are wearing some sort of burgundy outfit. We wear colors to set ourselves apart from the others, but we aren't doing that if everyone is wearing the same color.

Above all, you must keep yourself looking well-put together, but never wear anything to distract from the audition materials you are presenting. In this case, if there is any question, I always tell my students to err on the side of conservative dress.

Plunging necklines and too much skin for any gender can be a distraction. So ladies, that means you will want to cover your legs with hose or tights. I'm not only suggesting this for reasons of staying conservative, but for practicality reasons. You will be going through several weeks of intense dance auditions, and I will bet you my next year's salary that you will have at least one bruise on your leg that you don't want the judges to see.

Women should wear a dress or a skirt with a blouse. Jumpsuits are back in style and they are a perfect alternative if you are not comfortable with a dress or skirt. Pants are acceptable, of course, if your monologue requires you to roll around on the floor, or a skirt or dress would be prohibitive. Keep your shoes to a ballet flat, or a very low-heeled character shoe. Remember, if things can go wrong, they will. If you give yourself the opportunity to trip wearing a high heel, then you probably will, and we don't want that to happen in the audition room.

Men should be in dress pants and a button-down or polo, *tucked in,* with a belt. A nice sweater with dress pants or khakis is also very acceptable. For shoes, please go with a nice brown or black dress shoe, and wear dark socks. No white socks, and certainly no bare ankles/no socks. It has become trendy now to wear a Converse-style shoe with dress pants or suits, and this is not appropriate here. A special word of advice for gentlemen: check your hair throughout the day. Bring a brush, a comb, hair product, anything you need to keep your hair looking like you actually put some time into it. I will be at Unifieds again this year, and I swear to the Theatre Gods, if I see as many boys walking around with mussed-up hair as I have in the past, I will throw a copy of this book at them.

There will be times when you need to change from your audition clothes to your dance clothes very quickly, so whenever you can layer those clothes (ladies' dance tights under dresses, men's dance t-shirt under a sweater), I would plan for that.

Pick fabrics that travel well, and don't need a lot of ironing or upkeep. Stay away from cotton, linen, and silk. Keep accessories at a bare minimum. All of your clothes should fit *well*. They want to see the shape of your body, but nothing should be too tight, or too loose and baggy.

Simple stud earrings are ok, remove facial piercings, and no rings or long necklaces. Note: for dance auditions, no jewelry of any kind is acceptable. Keep your hair pulled back off your face, and make sure that any hair accessories are functional, and not decorative or distracting. If your nails are painted, they should be with clear or light pink polish only.

## Dance Audition Attire

Ladies should wear a colored leotard (please not black, burgundy, and NEVER white), with tan or flesh-tone tights, and tan shoes. Black shoes cut your leg off at the foot, as do footless tights. You will want to bring your ballet shoes (tan or pink), and soft-soled jazz shoes. Have your tan low-heeled character shoes on hand in case they ask you to wear them but sometimes they will not. Be sure to check the school's website if they ask for tap shoes, but most do not.
Bring SEVERAL pairs of tights. If your tights begin to look dingy, dirty, or discolored, please put on another pair and wash those out in your hotel room that night before you wear them again. You may bring a pair of jazz pants or a ballet skirt to wear over your outfit as well, if you are more comfortable wearing that, but remember, they want to see your body.

Men should wear black soft-soles jazz or ballet shoes, with form-fitting jazz pants and a tight colored shirt. Do not wear white, as it will look dirty quickly. If you are in very good shape, then a tight fitting tank and tights can work as well, or any combination that suits you (i.e. a t-shirt and tights, a tank and jazz pants).

Since I was a vocal major at Juilliard, I asked one of my dear friends and former Juilliard classmates who was a dance major to chime in on proper dance audition attire. Here's what Kristen Weiser, Ballet Master for Columbia Performing Arts Center had to say:

*"The best advice I ever got when it came to auditions was if you are unsure of what to wear, bring a few different outfits to the audition and look around when you arrive to see what most of the others are wearing, then wear the same. Also, do something small to stand out so they can remember you like putting a small braid in your hair before you put it in a bun, or find a leotard with an interesting cut. That way they when they are discussing you then can say 'Number 32 with... she was the one with the braid in her hair and the leotard with the extra straps on the back.' Make sure you wear the outfit that you look best in, and one that will be remembered."*

Lastly, and I can't stress this enough, bring at least one back-up regular outfit, and one back-up dance outfit. Drinks spill. Mud splashes. Seams rip. Birds poop. Expect the unexpected and be prepared for wardrobe malfunctions. For good examples of audition wardrobe choices, please visit The College Audition on Pinterest.

## What to Bring to Your Auditions

✓ Your audition wardrobe for each day, and your back-up audition outfit.

✓ Your dance clothes, and all dance shoes you need.

✓ Your binder of music, in sheet protectors, and clearly marked. Have other songs in your book in case they ask you for anything else. This happens more than you think.

✓ Your portable Bluetooth speaker to play your audition accompaniment. Bring extra batteries, the charger cable, AND a hard cable to hook your phone directly to the speaker in case there are problems connecting to Bluetooth in your audition.

✓ Copies of the script of the plays from where you chose your monologue. Re-read these plays in the car or on the plane.

✓ At least 50 copies of your headshot and resume, stapled. Store half of them in your binder, and half of them in your suitcase. Again, you never know what *might* happen, so you want to have backups.

✓ Pack your thank-you cards and stamps (more on this later).

✓ Water bottle

✓ Bring your copy of "The College Audition Workbook."

✓ At least 2-3 pens so you can fill out any paperwork when you get to the audition site.

## At the Audition

When you're at your auditions it is important to keep to yourself, and keep your head in the game. I saw this for two reasons. First, it is important to conserve your energy while you're at these auditions, and making friends, or hanging out with old friends that you may not have seen since summer camp sounds like it might be fun, but you don't want to distract yourself from the task at hand.

Unifieds, for example, take place in major cities with lots of shows and museums, and restaurants. Each night after your auditions, go back to your hotel room and rest. If you want to see that hot new Broadway show while you're in NYC, plan to do it on your last night of Unifieds, or stay an extra couple of days to explore the city you're in.

Second, remember that this is a competition, and it's not really the time to make new friends. This may sound like more harsh words from Tim, but the truth is, when large numbers of theatre kids get together it just becomes a big game of "who has the coolest resume," "who can name-drop the most," and just general one-upmanship. Hearing that the girl going in before you just came off the national tour of "Fun Home," or the boy after you was once told he sang well by Lin-Manuel Miranda will only frazzle you. You are there to show them who YOU are, and not be freaked out by who everyone else is.

When you arrive at the room to audition, take out your audition workbook and take notes of the people who are in the room to see you. This is where the Thank You cards come in. At the conclusion of each audition day, write a simple thank-you note of a few sentences to each person that was in the room, and address it to their name in care of (c/o) the school. The thank you note should be just three to four sentences, but it should include something in there that will make them remember you. Something personal you talked about, some advice they gave you, or something funny or awkward that may have happened in the room. It's important that you drop those notes in the mail the same day as the audition, so the odds are good that it will be waiting on their desk for them as soon as they get back to their office. This simple act of appreciation goes a long way, trust me.

## The Interview (Artistic Review)

After you have completed your audition pieces, there will be a short interview, which is sometimes called an "Artistic Review." This may happen immediately following your monologues and songs, or you may be called back into the room at a later time for this.

This is the time that the auditors will try to get to know you, as a person. This interview can be equally as important as showing them your acting, singing, and dancing abilities.

In order to be successful at your interview, you will have needed to do your research on the program ahead of time.

You will be expected to ask just as many questions of them as they are asking of you, and showing that you know the names of some of the faculty, famous alumni, and which shows they did recently will go a long way. Even if this is a Unified walk-up that you signed up for on the spot, go to their site on your phone and gather some basic information.

One question that I absolutely dread, and wish all colleges would banish from the interviews is "Which other colleges are you applying to?" While this may just be small talk, it tends to send students into a nervous mess. Be expecting the question, and be ready to give a rehearsed answer. Why rehearsed? Because I don't want you to tell them ANY of the other schools you are auditioning for.

The trick is finding a polite way around the answer. I always suggest a big smile and say "Right now, I can only think about auditioning for your school, and doing my best to present myself to you."
It seems cheesy, but you really are not required to answer the question for them. What is important that you show them you are confident, polite, and someone they want to work with.

## After the Audition

Now… exhale. It's over. You've done everything you could have, and you left your heart in that audition room. Now you're biggest question is "When will I hear!?"

Who knows. Most of the colleges will tell you when you can expect admissions decisions, but as a rule, some colleges with rolling admissions will let you know within two weeks of your audition date. The other programs will begin sending letters, emails, and making phone calls at then end of February, and usually conclude by the last week of March.

While you are waiting for the decisions to come in, and if you would like to keep your sanity, I would stay away from the online forums and social media. Also, do not post any acceptances to any college, and do not post about your audition experiences for any of them on any form of social media or public website. Someone you don't want to see it will see it. The just will. Trust me.

Only once you have chosen your school, and signed the paperwork, should you announce on social media that you have selected a college.

While you are waiting for your acceptance letters, know that you have a few rights and responsibilities, according to the National Association of College Admissions Counselors (remember them?) Please refer to Appendix D at the back of the book and read this list carefully.

As the list of acceptances and rejections come in, remember this:


# You will end up exactly where you are meant to be.

Now that you have the list of colleges to which you were accepted, you should have a few weeks before the May 1 signing deadline to visit these schools. Plan ahead in your schedule when you will have the time to do this even before you know where you are going.

When visiting the colleges, have your list of questions ready to go to ask while you are there. If possible, this is also your time to meet with the admissions office, and the financial aid office to make sure you are receiving the best financial aid packages available to you. In many cases, there is an appeal process in place to ask for more money from the school if you need to seek additional funds to make it work for you.

Once you have made your decision, you must contact the school and submit your paperwork immediately. On the other side, as soon as you are sure you don't want to attend a school that has accepted you, it is imperative that you notify the school immediately. Remember, there are students who are on the wait list who are anxiously awaiting a spot to open up.

If you find yourself on a waitlist for a school you would choose over a school that accepted you, it is in your best interest to proceed as though you did not get accepted to the wait list school. You will be notified by August 1 if you have been accepted to a wait-listed school. The money you have put down as a deposit on the other school will be forfeited, but that is a small price to pay to be accepted to the college of your dreams.

Finally, if you were not accepted to a school at all, or not accepted to any school where you feel you would be happy, you have the option to either take a gap year and re-audition, or take your first year of classes at another school, and re-apply the following year. In many cases as a BFA or BM student, you may have to start from square one as a freshman after you transfer, but as a BA student, your core classes will likely transfer with you.

Henry Ford once said "Failure is the opportunity to being again more intelligently." Take the year to double down on your training and improve your weaknesses and re-apply. One year is not the end of the world when it comes to ending up at the school where you will be happiest.

## A Final Word

I started this book with a question for you. Are you *absolutely sure* you want to commit your life to a degree in the performing arts? If, after reading through these pages, you are still absolutely sure this life is for you, then I have these words of encouragement for you:

Never give up. Keep fighting for what you are passionate, and you will end up where you are meant to be, and you will be happy there.

# A
# DIRECTORY OF SUMMER PROGRAMS

*The following director of Summer Programs is a comprehensive, but not a complete list.*

## Pre-College Programs

| | |
|---|---|
| California State Summer School for the Arts | CA |
| Notre Dame de Namur Univ. - Music Theatre Conservatory | CA |
| University of Southern California - Summer Theatre Conservatory | CA |
| UCLA - Summer Acting and Performance Institute | CA |

| | |
|---|---|
| Wesleyan College - Center for Creative Youth | CT |
| Yale University – Summer Conservatory for Actors | CT |
| Georgetown University – US Performing Arts Camps | DC |
| Northwestern University – The Cherubs | IL |
| Indiana University – College Audition Preparation | IN |
| Berklee College of Music – Musical Theater Intensive | MA |
| Boston Conservatory – Musical Theatre Dance Intensive | MA |
| Boston University – Summer Theatre Institute | MA |
| Emerson College | MA |
| University of Michigan – Mpulse Performing Arts Institutes | MI |
| MUNY – Webster | MO |
| North Carolina School of the Arts – Summer Session | NC |

| | |
|---|---|
| University of North Carolina School of the Arts – Drama Summer Intensive | NC |
| Rider University – Westminster Music Theatre Workshop | NJ |
| Rutgers University – Summer Acting Conservatory | NJ |
| CAP 21 High School Musical Theatre Training | NY |
| Fordham University – Summer Musical Theatre Intensive | NY |
| Ithaca College – Introduction to Musical Theatre Performance | NY |
| Marymount Manhattan – Musical Theatre Precollege Summer Intensive | NY |
| NYU Steinhardt – NYU Summer Study in Music Theatre | NY |
| NYU Tisch School of the Arts – Summer High School | NY |
| Pace Summer Scholars | NY |
| SUNY Purchase – Precollege Programs in the Arts | NY |
| Syracuse University Summer College – Acting and Musical Theatre Program | NY |
| Wagner College – Summer Music Theatre Institute | NY |

| | |
|---|---|
| Baldwin Wallace, Music Theatre Overtures | OH |
| Oklahoma City University – High School Musical Theatre Program | OK |
| Carnegie Mellon University School of Drama Pre-College Program | PA |
| Penn State School of Theatre | PA |
| University of the Arts – Summer Institute | PA |
| Brown University – TheatreBridge | RI |
| Texas State University | TX |

## Summer Programs

| | |
|---|---|
| American Conservatory Theater | CA |
| Idyllwild Arts Teens & Kids Summer Program | CA |
| Musical Theatre University | CA |
| Perry-Mansfield Performing Arts Camp | CO |
| Buck's Rock Creative and Performing Arts Camp | CT |
| Broadway Theatre Project | FL |

| | |
|---|---|
| Broward Center for the Performing Arts | FL |
| The Broadway Theatre Project | FL |
| The Dr. Philips Center for the Performing Arts | FL |
| The Patel Conservatory | FL |
| Broadway Dreams Foundation | GA |
| Walnut Hill School Summer Theater | MA |
| Interlochen Arts Camp | MI |
| Arts Bridge Summer Musical Theatre | MN |
| The Performing Arts Project (TPAP) | NC |
| AMDA - High School Summer Conservatory | NY |
| Broadway Artist Alliance | NY |
| Camp Broadway | NY |
| Circle in the Square Theater School | NY |
| Columbia University Theatrical Collaboration | NY |
| French Woods Festival | NY |
| Lee Strasberg Institute | NY |

| | |
|---|---|
| Long Lake Arts Camp | NY |
| Making It on Broadway Intensives | NY |
| Open Jar Institute | NY |
| Stage Door Manor | NY |
| Stella Adler Studio | NY |
| The Broadway Workshop | NY |
| TripleArts | NY |
| Cleveland Musical Theatre | OH |
| UC College Conservatory of Music High School MT Workshop | OH |
| Southeastern Summer Theatre Institute | SC |
| Dallas Summer Musicals College Weekend | TX |
| TexArts | TX |

# B
# DIRECTORY OF COLLEGES

*The following directory of college programs has been compiled to the best of my knowledge. It is a comprehensive list, though not a complete list. It is imperative that you check each school's website for accurate and up-to-date information, and not rely solely on this list while making your decisions. It is provided here only as a guide and starting point.*

## Reach Schools

| | | |
|---|---|---|
| University of Arizona | BFA (MT), BA (Th) | AZ |
| California State University - Fullerton | BFA (MT), BA (Th) | CA |
| University of California - Los Angeles (UCLA) | BA (Th) | CA |

| | | |
|---|---|---|
| University of California - Berkeley | BA (Th) | CA |
| University of Southern California | BFA Acting, MT Minor | CA |
| University of Hartford, The Hartt School of Music | BFA | CT |
| Yale University | BA (Th) | CT |
| Florida State University | BFA, BM, BA (Th) | FL |
| University of Central Florida | BFA | FL |
| University of Miami | BFA, BM, BA (Th) | FL |
| DePaul University | BFA | IL |
| Northwestern University | BA (Th), BM (MT) | IL |
| Roosevelt University | BFA | IL |

| | | |
|---|---|---|
| Boston Conservatory | BFA | MA |
| Emerson College | BFA | MA |
| Harvard University | BA (Th) | MA |
| University of Michigan - Ann Arbor | BFA, BA (Th) | MI |
| Webster University | BFA | MO |
| Duke University | BA (Th) | NC |
| Elon University | BFA | NC |
| University of North Carolina, Chapel Hill | BA Drama, BM (MT) | NC |
| Dartmouth College | BA | NH |
| Princeton University | BA (Th) | NJ |

| | | |
|---|---|---|
| Columbia University/Barnard | BA (Acting/Theatre Arts) | NY |
| Ithaca College | BFA (Th, MT, Acting) | NY |
| NYU Steinhardt | BM (MT) | NY |
| NYU Tisch | BFA (MT, Th) | NY |
| Pace University | BFA (MT), BA (Th) | NY |
| Syacuse Univeristy | BFA (MT, Acting) | NY |
| The Juilliard School | BFA (Acting) | NY |
| Baldwin Wallace University | BM (MT) | OH |
| Otterbein College | BFA (MT) | OH |
| University of Cincinnati "CCM" | BFA (MT, Acting) | OH |

| | | |
|---|---|---|
| Oklahoma City University | BFA (MT, Acting), BA, BM) | OK |
| University of Oklahoma | BFA (MT, Acting) | OK |
| Carnegie-Mellon University | BFA (MT, Acting) | PA |
| Penn State University | BFA (MT), BA (Acting) | PA |
| Point Park University | BFA (MT, A), BA (A) | PA |
| University of the Arts | BFA (MT, A), BA (A) | PA |
| Brown University | BA (Th) | RI |
| Sam Houston State University | BFA (MT, Acting) | TX |
| Texas State University | BFA (MT, A) | TX |
| Shenandoah Conservatory | BFA (MT, A) | VA |

| University of Wisconsin, Stevens Point | BFA (MT) | WI |
|---|---|---|

## Target Schools

| Auburn University | BFA | AL |
|---|---|---|
| Birmingham-Southern College | BA | AL |
| Samford University | BA | AL |
| University of Mobile | BM | AL |
| Arizona State University | BA (Th), BM (MT) | AZ |
| Chapman University | BFA Acting | CA |
| Loyola Marymount University | BA Acting | CA |
| Notre Dame de Namur University | BA | CA |

| | | |
|---|---|---|
| Pepperdine University | BA | CA |
| Redlands University | BA | CA |
| University of California - Davis | BA | CA |
| University of California - Irvine | BA, BFA | CA |
| University of Colorado at Boulder | BFA (MT), BA (Th) | CO |
| University of Colorado at Denver | BA (Th), BFA (Th) | CO |
| University of Denver | BA (Th) | CO |
| University of Northern Colorado | BA | CO |
| American University | BA | DC |
| Catholic University | BM (MT) | DC |

| | | |
|---|---|---|
| Howard University | BFA | DC |
| Jacksonville University | BA, BFA, BM, BS | FL |
| New World School of the Arts | BFA (AA also offered) | FL |
| Palm Beach Atlantic University | BA | FL |
| Rollins College | BA (Th) w/ MT Concentration | FL |
| University of Florida | BA, BFA, BM | FL |
| University of Tampa | BA | FL |
| Savannah College of Art and Design | BFA | GA |
| Shorter College | BFA | GA |
| Valdosta University | BFA | GA |

| | | |
|---|---|---|
| Drake University | BFA | IA |
| University of Idaho | BFA | ID |
| Illinois State University | BA | IL |
| Illinois Wesleyan University | BA (Th), BFA (MT) | IL |
| Milikin University | BFA | IL |
| North Central College | BA | IL |
| Rockford College | BFA | IL |
| Southern Illinois University - Carbondale | BFA | IL |
| Western Illinois University | BFA | IL |
| Ball State University | BFA | IN |

| | | |
|---|---|---|
| Indiana University at Bloomington | BFA | IN |
| University of Kansas | BFA | KS |
| Tulane University | BFA, BA (Th) | LA |
| Boston University | BFA (Th) | MA |
| Northeastern University | BM | MA |
| Goucher College | BA (Th) | MD |
| Towson University | BA (Th), BS (Th) | MD |
| University of Maryland - Baltimore County | BA, BFA (Th) | MD |
| University of Maryland - College Park | BA (Th) | MD |
| University of Southern Maine | BM | ME |

| | | |
|---|---|---|
| Adrien College | BA | MI |
| Central Michigan University | BFA | MI |
| Eastern Michigan University | BF (Th), BS (Th), MT Minor | MI |
| Michigan State University | BA (Th) | MI |
| Oakland University | BFA, BA (Th) | MI |
| University of Michigan - Flint | BFA (Th) | MI |
| Western Michigan University | BFA | MI |
| Culver Stockton College | BFA | MO |
| Lindenwood College | BFA | MO |
| Missouri State University | BFA | MO |

| | | |
|---|---|---|
| Missouri Valley College | BFA | MO |
| Southwest Missouri State | BFA | MO |
| University of Missouri - Kansas City | BA | MO |
| Catawba College | BFA, BA | NC |
| East Carolina University | BFA | NC |
| Lees-McRae College | BFA | NC |
| Mars Hill College | BFA | NC |
| Western Carolina University | BFA, BM | NC |
| University of North Dakota | BFA | ND |
| University of Nebraska at Kearney | BFA | NE |

| | | |
|---|---|---|
| Plymouth State University | BFA | NH |
| Drew University | BA (Th) | NJ |
| Fairleigh Dickinson University | BA | NJ |
| Kean University | BFA, BA (Th) | NJ |
| Monthclair State University | BFA (MT), BA (Th) | NJ |
| Rider University | BFA (MT, Th), BA (Th) | NJ |
| Rowan University | BA (Th) | NJ |
| Rutgers University Camden | BA (Th) | NJ |
| Rutgers University New Brunswick | BFA, BA (Th) | NJ |
| Seton Hall University | BA (Th) | NJ |

| | | |
|---|---|---|
| Westminster College of the Arts at Rider | BFA (MT) | NJ |
| William Patterson University | BA, BM | NJ |
| Santa Fe University of Art and Design | BFA (MT) | NM |
| University of Nevada - Reno | BA (Th), BFA (MT) | NV |
| Adelphi University | BFA (Th) | NY |
| American Academy of Dramatic Arts (AMDA) | Certificate/BFA | NY |
| Circle in the Square Theatre | Certificate | NY |
| Colgate University | BA (Th) | NY |
| Five Towns College | BFA (Th, MT) | NY |
| Fordham University | BA (Th) | NY |

| | | |
|---|---|---|
| Hofstra University | BA, BFA (Th, MT) | NY |
| Hunter College, CUNY | BA (Th) | NY |
| Long Island University, CW Post | BFA (Th, MT) | NY |
| Manhattanville College | BA (MT, Th) | NY |
| Marymount Manhattan | BFA, BA (MT, Th) | NY |
| Molloy College/CAP 21 | BFA (MT, Th) | NY |
| Nazareth College | BA (Th) | NY |
| Russell Sage College | BS | NY |
| SUNY Buffalo | BFA (MT, Acting), BA (Th) | NY |
| SUNY Cortland | BA (MT minor) | NY |

| | | |
|---|---|---|
| SUNY Fredonia | BFA (MT) | NY |
| SUNY Geneseo | BA (Th) | NY |
| SUNY Purchase | BFA (Acting), BA (Th) | NY |
| The New School | BFA, BA | NY |
| Vassar College | BA | NY |
| Wagner College | BA (MT, Acting) | NY |
| Ashland University | BA (Th) | OH |
| Bowling Green State University | BA (MT Concentration) | OH |
| Heidelberg University | BA, BS (Th, MT Conc.) | OH |
| Kent State | BFA (MT) | OH |

| | | |
|---|---|---|
| Marietta College | BFA, BA | OH |
| Ohio Northern University | BFA | OH |
| University of Akron | BA | OH |
| Wright State | BFA (MT, Acting) | OH |
| Youngstown State University | BFA (MT) | OH |
| University of Central Oklahoma | BM (MT) | OK |
| University of Tulsa | BA (MT minor) | OK |
| Southern Oregon University | BFA (Th, MT Minor) | OR |
| Clarion University | BFA | PA |
| Coastal Carolina University | BFA (MT, A), BA (Th) | SC |

| | | |
|---|---|---|
| Coker College | BFA (MT) | SC |
| Limestone College | BFA (MT) | SC |
| University of South Dakota | BFA | SD |
| Belmont University | BM, BFA (MT, A) | TN |
| University of Memphis | BFA (Th, MT conc.) | TN |
| Abilene Christian University | BFA (MT, A) | TX |
| Southwestern University | BFA (Th, MT Conc.) | TX |
| Texas Christian University | BFA (MT) | TX |
| University of Texas at Arlington | BM (MT) | TX |
| University of Texas at El Paso | BFA (MT, A) | TX |

| | | |
|---|---|---|
| Brigham Young University | BA | UT |
| University of Utah | BFA (MT, A) | UT |
| Virginia Commonwealth University | BFA (Performance) | VA |
| Central Washington University | BFA (MT, A) | WA |
| Cornish College of the Arts | BFA (MT conc) | WA |
| Viterbo University | BFA (MT, A) | WI |
| University of Wyoming | BFA | WY |

## Safety Schools

| | | |
|---|---|---|
| University of South Alabama | BFA | AL |
| Ouachita Baptist University | BM | AR |
| California State University - Chico | BA | CA |

| | | |
|---|---|---|
| California State University - Northridge | BA (Th) with MT minor | CA |
| Santa Clara University | BA (Th) with MT minor | CA |
| Metropolitan State College of Denver | BFA | CO |
| Western Connecticut State University | BA | CT |
| University of West Florida | BA, BFA | FL |
| Brenau University | BFA | GA |
| Columbia College | BA, BFA | IL |
| Friends University | BA | KS |
| Wichita State University | BFA | KS |
| Northern Kentucky University | BFA | KY |

| | | |
|---|---|---|
| Western Kentucky University | BFA | KY |
| Northwestern State University | BS | LA |
| Brandeis University | BA | MA |
| University of Minnesota - Duluth | BFA | MN |
| Avila University | BFA | MO |
| Stephens College | BFA | MO |
| University of Mississippi | BFA | MS |
| University of Southern Mississippi | BFA | MS |
| Meredith College | BA | NC |
| Nebraska Wesleyan | BFA | NE |

| University of New Hampshire | BA (Th) w/MT Minor | NH |
|---|---|---|
| University of Nevada - Las Vegas | BA | NV |
| DeSales University | BA | PA |
| Marywood University | BA | PA |
| Muhlenberg College | BA | PA |
| Seton Hill University | BA (Th) | PA |
| Susquehanna University | BA (Th, MT concentration) | PA |
| Temple University | BA (Th) | PA |
| University of Pennsylvania | BA (Theatre Arts) | PA |
| West Chester University | BA (Th) | PA |

| | | |
|---|---|---|
| Wilkes University | BA | PA |
| Rhode Island College | BA (Th) | RI |
| Northern State University | BA | SD |
| St. Edward's University | BA (MT Conc.) | TX |
| West Texas A&M | BA (Th) | TX |
| Southern Utah University | BFA (Th, MT Conc.) | UT |
| Weber State University | BA, BS (Th) | UT |
| Barter Conservatory at Emory | BA (MT) | VA |
| Christopher Newport University | BA (Th, MT Conc.) | VA |
| College of William and Mary | BA (Th) | VA |

| | | |
|---|---|---|
| James Madison University | BA (MT, A) BM | VA |
| University of Virginia | BA (Th) | VA |
| University of Richmond | BA (Th) | VA |
| Johnson State College | BA (Th) | VT |
| University of Puget Sound | BA (Th) | WA |
| University of Washington | BA (MT/A) | WA |
| University of Wisconsin, Green Bay | BA (MT, A) | WI |
| West Virginia Wesleyan College | BA (Th, MT Minor) | WV |

# C
# LINKS AND OTHER RESOURCES

**www.thecollegeaudition.com**
The College Audition. Book private coaching sessions, contact Tim Evanicki, and visit The College Audition Store for more resources.

**www.thevocaltechnician.com**
My private voice studio website. Follow my blog for valuable information on singing, song selection, finding a voice teacher, and more!

**www.getacceptd.com**
Acceptd. Sign up for an account on this website to submit your prescreen auditions and sign up for audition times.

**www.collegeconfidential.com**

College Confidential. A forum website where you can exchange ideas and research with other students and parents on the college audition process.

**www.performerstuff.com**

Performer Stuff. A great resource to find audition material including monologues and song cuts.

**www.broadwayartistsalliance.com**

A wonderful training program in NYC offering single-day and multi-day workshops and camps with Broadway professionals, and casting directors.

**www.youngarts.org**

A non-profit organization in South Florida that offers workshops, programming, and scholarships. The signature event each year is YoungArts Week.

**www.theatre-schools.com**

A fabulous resource/search engine for finding theatre schools and programs online, in one place.

**www.unifiedauditions.com**

The National Unified Auditions, taking place each year in New York, Chicago, and Los Angeles, where dozens of schools come together in one place to hold auditions.

**www.nacacnet.org**

The quintessential Performing Arts College Fair. A must-attend for all future college students pursuing a performing arts degree.

**www.wetorangestudio.com**

Hands down, my first recommendation for college headshots in Florida.

# D
# STUDENT RIGHTS AND RESPONSIBILITIES
## ACCORDING TO THE NATIONAL ASSOCIATION FOR COLLEGE ADMISSION COUNSELORS

### Colleges Must Provide:

### General:
• The cost of attending an institution, including tuition, books and supplies, housing, and related costs and fees
• Requirements and procedures for withdrawing from an institution, including refund policies
• Names of associations that accredit, approve or license the institution
• Special facilities and services for disabled students.

### Academics:

- The academic program of the institution, including degrees, programs of study, and facilities
- A list of faculty and other instructional personnel • A report on completion or graduation rates at the college
- At schools that typically prepare students for transfer to a four-year college, such as a community college, information about the transfer- out rate.

## Financial Aid:

- The types of financial aid, including federal, state and local government, need-based and non-need based, and private scholarships and awards
- The methods by which a school determines eligibility for financial aid; how and when the aid is distributed
- Terms and conditions of campus employment, if financial aid is delivered through a work-study aid program.

For more information about student financial aid, visit www.studentaid.gov.

Campus Security:

- Procedures and policies for reporting crimes and emergencies on campus, as well as the system of adjudication
- The number and types of crime reported on and around campus
- The school's drug offense policy, as well as descriptions of the school's drug awareness and drug use prevention programs.

To compare campus crime statistics for different colleges, visit http://ope.ed.gov/security.

## STUDENT RIGHTS

### Before You Apply:
• You have the right to receive factual and comprehensive information from colleges and universities about their admission, financial costs, aid opportunities, practices and packaging policies, and housing policies. If you consider applying under an early admission plan, you have the right to complete information from the college about its process and policies.
• You have the right to be free from high-pressure sales tactics.

### When You Are Offered Admission:
• You have the right to wait until May 1 to respond to an offer of ad- mission and/or financial aid.
• Colleges that request commitments to offers of admission and/or financial assistance prior to May 1 must clearly offer you the opportunity to request (in writing) an extension until May 1. They must grant you this extension and your request may not jeopardize your status for admission and/or financial aid.
• Candidates admitted under early decision programs are a recognized exception to the May 1 deadline.

### If You Are Placed on a Wait/Alternate List:
• The letter that notifies you of that placement should provide a history that describes the number of students on the wait list, the number offered admission, and the availability of financial aid and housing.
• Colleges may require neither a deposit nor a written commitment as a condition of remaining on a wait list.

- Colleges are expected to notify you of the resolution of your wait list status by August 1 at the latest.

## STUDENT RESPONSIBILITIES

### Before You Apply:
- You have a responsibility to research, and to understand and com- ply with the policies and procedures of each college or university regarding application fees, financial aid, scholarships, and housing. You should also be sure you understand the policies of each college or university regarding deposits you may be required to make before you enroll.

### As You Apply:
- You must complete all material required for application and submit your application on or before the published deadlines. You should be the sole author of your applications.
- You should seek the assistance of your high school counselor early and throughout the application period. Follow the process recom- mended by your high school for filing college applications.
- It is your responsibility to arrange, if appropriate, for visits to and/or interviews at colleges of your choice.

### After You Receive Your Admission Decisions:
- You must notify each college or university that accepts you whether you are accepting or rejecting its offer. You should make these notifications as soon as you have made a final decision as to the college you wish to attend, but no later than May 1. It is understood that May 1 will be the postmark date.

• You may confirm your intention to enroll and, if required, submit a deposit to only one college or university. The exception to this arises if you are put on a wait list by a college or university and are later admitted to that institution. You may accept the offer and send a deposit. However, you must immediately notify a college or university at which you previously indicated your intention to enroll.

• If you are accepted under an early decision plan, you must promptly withdraw the applications submitted to other colleges and universities and make no additional applications. If you are an early decision candidate and are seeking financial aid, you need not withdraw other applications until you have received notification about financial aid.

If you think your rights have been denied, you should contact the college or university immediately to request additional information or the extension of a reply date. In addition, you should ask your counselor to notify the president of the state or regional affiliate of the National Association for College Admission Counseling in your area. If you need further assistance, send a copy of any correspondence you have had with the college or university and a copy of your letter of admission to:

National Association for College Admission Counseling
1631 Prince Street Alexandria, VA 22314-2818
Phone: 703/836-2222 800/822-6285
Fax: 703/ 836-8015 www.nacacnet.org

# CONNECT WITH TIM EVANICKI AND THE COLLEGE AUDITION!

Please visit my website at www.thecollegeaudition.com and sign up for my mailing list. Or visit my personal website, www.timevanicki.com, for booking me as a master class clinician or speaker.

Also, don't forget to follow me on Facebook, Twitter, Instagram, and YouTube!

Made in the USA
Columbia, SC
05 June 2018